June 2024
ISBN-979-8-9855592-6-2

END IN LIGHT

SELECTED POEMS

JEFFREY CHARLES
KINARD

To Anika

END IN LIGHT

END IN LIGHT
SELECTED POEMS

CHILD OF THE RIVER

Riding along
in the river
meander

Knowing the world
in the present
encounter

Swift as a stream
in the depths
of the narrows

Finding a way
around any
obstruction

Full of desire
life longs to touch us
All of the world
craves our attention
Child of the river
let your life have you

Child of the river
let your life have you

B E W I L D E R E D

Did you have a childhood
of magic
Reckless abandon
in the woods?

Was it you remember
who chased down
every shadow not
understood?

Do you ever wander
bewildered
across the concrete
in a dream?

Do you ever stare at
the symbols
Wonder exactly
what they mean?

> The sun's not going down
> The earth is spinning 'round
> The light it does not leave
> It's we who turn away

All of these vibrations
to reach me
Seek and find
the way in

Echoes sound familiar
but lost it
The wisp of spider
web ascends

I crave a deeper blue
adventure
A twilight of trees
in the wind

Here is where I'll draw
my circle
My last stand begins
at the end

> The sun's not going down
> The earth is spinning 'round
> The light it does not leave
> It's we who turn away

Sometimes I feel dizzy
I let go
What will be will be
without me

I will pay attention
to rhythms
Dream the dream of ships
lost at sea

Do you ever wander
bewildered
across the concrete
in a dream?

Did you have a childhood
of magic
where nothing ever
feels complete?

Not Dying

I'm not dying
Not dying today
I'm awaking
The past was a dream

I am in love
with thresholds again
I am in love
with transformations

       I am collected now
       I am whole
       I am crafting brand new
       dice to roll

       I am filled with light
       My woes are few
       I am stronger than before
       I am renewed

I am melting
I'm melting away
In the silence
my thoughts are a dream

I'm arriving
Arriving in waves
I'm not dying
Not dying today

WHERE NOTHING HURTS

When I do not have a song
When I'm done with pretty words
When my eyes become as dull
as the eyes of a dead bird

    Drop me down a deep dark well
    Dry as my mouth has become
    I don't want to live forever
    Give the parched earth back it's blood

When I no longer feel the world
Lost every hair upon my skin
When I'm finished looking for
the door where I came in

    Moon take me with you
    into the shadows for a spell
    I don't want to live forever
    and I promise not to tell

When I do not have a song
When I'm done with pretty words
I know I will return
to the place where nothing hurts

Running Away

Wild were the trees
Lost in the sway
Clouds on the breeze
We ran away

Far from the streets
On summer days
Soil on our feet
We ran away

> Summer skies
> near the stream
> and the willows

> Where we dreamed
> with the grass
> as our pillow

Dark were the skies
Love was a maze
We couldn't stop
We ran away

Where are you now?
Still on your way?
I'm still in love
with running away

> Summer skies
> near the stream
> and the willows

Where we dreamed
with the grass
as our pillow

Oh, what dreams we had
What joy in running mad

Wild were the trees
Lost in the sway
Clouds on the breeze
We ran away

THE FLAT EARTH

There's supposed to be
a mountain here
With peaks so high
you'll disappear
to another
atmosphere
Where has the mountain gone?

Between the desert
and the sea
I got lost
among the trees
The river swelled
from marsh to swamp
Where has the mountain gone?

There's supposed to be
a mountain here
With peaks so high
you'll disappear
to another
atmosphere
Where has the mountain gone?

I turned around
Went the other way
Followed the river
past a thousand streams
I found the wounds
where the earth bleeds
Where has the mountain gone?

There's supposed to be
a mountain here
With peaks so high
you'll disappear
to another
atmosphere
Where has the mountain gone?

The flat earth
has been ground down
From mountains
into tiny mounds
Storms now blow
the dust around
The mountains are all gone

I Didn't Die

I didn't die
At times I meant to
And I didn't like
saying goodbye
    to the best in me

I will not lie
I see no need to
inflate my pride
I still decide
    what to live up to

        I am hollow
        muted nightfall
        I am heat death
        waiting for dew point
        Holding my breath
        I am awful
        I am background radiation

I just get by
while learning how to
bring my insides
out into the light
    until I'm see-through

I didn't die
At times I meant to
And I didn't like
saying goodbye
    to the best in me

S HIPWRECKS

Winter's eve
The moon in Scorpio
I met a stranger
Stranger than I know

In a spell
the sun lit up the night
Two tangled lovers
steaming in the ice

Barely hello
and we're saying goodbye
Shipwrecks passing in the night
I know I know
Didn't mean a thing
It didn't mean a thing
Barely hello

No one knows
how deep the darkness goes
But I'm gonna dive
Gonna dive alone

Let me go
You can just close the door
I won't come around
Not anymore

Barely hello
and we're saying goodbye
Shipwrecks passing in the night
I know I know
Didn't mean a thing
It didn't mean a thing
Barely hello

NO MORE GOODBYES

No more goodbyes
for no more lovers
I just watch them
drift away

I carry on
doing what I'm doing
They come and go
They've yet to stay

       I'm having a hard time
       knowing a partner
       Someone who fits
       from day to day

       So far I always
       change to receive them
       I've not the will
       to stay that way

Rather than love
I will know lonely
Maybe they are
one in the same

No more goodbyes
for no more lovers
I just watch them
drift away

SWEETHEARTS

We are sweethearts
Giggling men
Been down to hell
Climbed out again

We love rainbows
Flowers in Spring
Better than the blood
when they tore off our wings

Have a smile now
for each soul we meet
We've known so much pain
It's a secret we keep

Love to help you
Shake hands as we leave
Thank you's the music
that soothes the gray beast

We are sweethearts
Look deep in our eyes
You'll see the abyss
where our innocence died

Amphibian

There's light dancing in libations
I'm on a liquid vacation
All my senses blurring in the din

Belly up to the log
feeling like a cross-eyed frog
The bar is full of flies
I'll never meet

There's syrup pouring out the speakers
Lizards laughing in the bleachers
Someone whispers I begin to spin

I'm here waiting for the urge
to step back and submerge
Drift into the dark
and fall asleep

A witch doctor with his shakers
fiddles with my inner nature
til I wonder which world I am in

Sitting neck deep in the pond
while the snapping turtles yawn
The bubbles bring
the swamp gas of relief

Are you in
with amphibians?
Can you swim
out of reach?

Belly up to the log
feeling like a cross-eyed frog
The bar is full of flies
I'll never meet

Animal

I'm an animal
Irrespectable
I let my tongue out
She's gonna follow me home

I'm an animal
Doused in chemicals
Teeth are sharper now
I'm a beast prowling alone

       Drank the fresh ocean
       Replaced it with tears
       Carved the lone mountain
       Been heartless for years

       When anyone smiles
       I look to the sun
       You don't want me
       I'm not the one

I'm an animal
Imperceptible
Senses inform
electric flesh encased in bone

I'm an animal
It's incredible
I dance in the blind
with all else upon this stone

THE END OF SUMMER

You wait in the shadows
She has a swagger in her approach
She feels so naked under her clothes

She wants to touch you
Feel the smooth warmth of your skin
Don't want her to stop once she begins

> She whispers sweet nothings in your ear
> Knowing her promises all disappear
> Do you really mind
> you never get what you expect?
> Just another beautiful wreck

Watch her walk away
She knows she leads you with her hips
She sees the kiss waiting on your lips

It's the end of summer
A hint of fall is in the air
She's trouble, but why should you care?

> She whispers sweet nothings in your ear
> Knowing her promises all disappear
> Do you really mind
> you never get what you expect?
> Just another beautiful wreck

H E A T

Such a dirty girl
I could fall into your hungry world
I am aching
and lost in the night

My dick is crazy
Such a sexy wife
I might just slide along
and end my life

Feels like a turn
I'm tempted to take
If I touch your hips
it would be a mistake

I can feel the static
when we stand too close
Promising lightning and thunder
Explode

We're already naked
Attached at the mouth
Clawing our skins
until the heat comes out

IN A NOWHERE PLACE

I don't know what to do
It's early still and I'm not with you
The buildings crumble like my face
While I'm at peace
in a nowhere place

I'm on a lonely plane
Soaring high belly full of flames
My skull gently touches outer space
While I'm at peace
in a nowhere place

I knew the water cool
King of slumber, ace of fools
The light was so fast I still gave chase
While I'm at peace
in a nowhere place

I'm going far away
Deep within on a power play
Nothing left to guide me but my grace
While I'm at peace
in a nowhere place

> And you'd be wrong
> If you assume what's going on
> And you'd be wrong
> If you think anything at all
> And you'd be wrong
> If you ever think you'll see me again

Not Happening

Oh, baby, that's okay
I'm not gonna play
with you tonight

Have another drink
Try not to get deep
You're never right

Oh, baby, I don't lie
Like your smoky eyes
Your pants so tight

Having too much fun
living on the run
It serves me right

    I'm just not that interested
    I'm not giving into it
    I'm already ripped to shreds
    That's what's happening
    Not happening

Oh, baby, when you're near
like gazing in a mirror
The appetite

Just a little touch
might prove to be too much
and we'd ignite

Do It for Darkness

Do it for darkness
Do it to fall
down off your high horse
once and for all

Do it for shadows
Do it to die
Release the dragon
protecting the lie

    I've got a present
    wrapped up for you
    A mouthful of venom
    ready to spew

    I've got a dagger
    aimed at my eye
    Made from the mirror
    I mistake for outside

        Look at us
        We are not silhouettes
        Look at us
        We are not silhouettes
        Look at us
        We are not silhouettes

Do it for darkness
Do it in time
to toast our good fortune
Our last glass of wine

S T O I C

I'll take the poverty
Pain and hardships unto me
I'll remain alone
if it's meant to be
Unless I let myself down

I want the mastery
Be complete as I can be
I am nothing else
I am just me
Unless I let myself down

> The loneliest bird
> soars high above the plains
> Adrift upon the winds
> None know the name

> Born of the clouds
> Destined not to land
> The loneliest bird
> knows no one understands

I will reach what I can touch
You do you and I will watch
We each decide
if we'll be just
Unless I let myself down

Write my life anew each day
Etch in stone mistakes I've made
Today I am
as I behave
Unless I let myself down

The loneliest bird
soars high above the plains
Adrift upon the winds
None know the name

Born of the clouds
Destined not to land
The loneliest bird
knows no one understands

I will die right on this spot
then pretend I'm what I'm not
I do not seek
what's not my lot
Unless I let myself down

Know my nature, know my rules
Know best how to ply my tools
Whether I be king
or I be fool
Unless I let myself down

BRIDGE MEN

And in the vacuum
The scraps and feathers
The dust and debris
of a dozen centuries

The last man laughing
Horny and thirsty
Delights in the sights
Falls in love with pretty lights

> But not us
> We are bridge men
> No longer human
> Drawing lightning from the sky
> Laying the cobbles as we die

> We are bridge men
> Pushing across the great divide
> Beasts of burden with wild eyes
> We are bridge men
> No longer human

We speak of nothing
They cannot hear us
Must be on our way
There is no one we can save

They look for only
a hand to soothe them
Safety and pleasure
as if they'll live forever

THREE-LEGGED DOG

I go
where my stumbling
takes my ego

It don't
make much difference
I got no home

No one ever tells me to stay
No one ever tells me to stay
They just want me off of their lawn
Three-legged dog

I know
I was born to travel
Even though

I got
one foot in the grave
and three to go

No one ever tells me to stay
No one ever tells me to stay
They just want me off of their lawn
Three-legged dog

I'm gonna climb up the mountain
I'm gonna sleep in the meadow
I'm gonna watch the sunrise
until I am supernatural

No one ever told me to stay
No one ever told me to stay
No one's gonna bury my bones
Three-legged dog

THE END OF OCTOBER

It's the end of October
and the rain is all but over
Dripping from the trees full of dead leaves

And the water in the street
runs in rivers to the sea
And that is where I crave to be right now

While the new moon's in the sky
I can escape on the king tide
Leaving all the crowded bars behind

For the sea that I was born
Never quite right when I'm ashore
Just too many rules, too many lines

       Being lost is for the rational
       The rest of us won't presume to know
       We take our ships to sea
       and do our best to read
       this mad world as it is happening
       Being lost, that ain't a thing

It's the end of October
My worries are all but over
Without the old burdens I am free

To the vastness cast my nets
Never know what I will get
I like the possibilities

THERE IS SOMETHING

There is something
Always something
I forget
from before

I don't love you
like I loved you
anymore

As the days spiral away
paths disappear in the haze
Things I do become things I've done
Those I love become those I've loved

In the moonlight
Bone white moonlight
I drift off
from the shore

I don't need you
No longer need you
anymore

There is little I can hold
Keep too much and I feel old
Let it pass -- there's more to come
Riding once more 'round the sun

1 9 9 4

I know you're somewhere
back there
Nineteen ninety-four

Along the highway
while they
race toward something more

They do not see you
hurting
Crawling from the door

You will be stronger
after
Nineteen ninety-four

> Did I see
> the untouched dreams
> rise into the sky?
> Lighting up the endless darkness
> in the corner of my eye
>
> Now I see
> you appear to me
> places you were before
> Up until the end of
> nineteen ninety-four

I don't believe you
when you
tell me that you're here

Until I see your
contours
slowly reappear

Among the shadows
where you
lost yourself before

There are no dead ends
my friend
Nineteen ninety-four

H A U N T   M E

Haunt me as I wander
rudderless upon the tide
I only speak to you
the only one who's by my side

I do not feel the same
as I did when we were alive
The world is so much smaller
with nothing to decide

> Haunt me I'm hollow
> and lost without my friend
> Haunt me on the waters
> until I see you again

Surrounded by deep waters
I've forgotten how to sleep
Haunt me never leave me
You're the company I keep

Let me hear your whisper
I will share this life with you
Until we are together
in forever very soon

> Haunt me I'm hollow
> and lost without my friend
> Haunt me on the waters
> until I see you again

DOWN FOR DAYS

Down for days
sleeping in the meadow
Breathing in the green grass of home

Skies of blue
and fragrant blooms of yellow
Good times often come from time alone

> On and on
> It feels like forever
> Waiting on the wind
> and the cold

> On and on
> Churning pain to pleasure
> Saying fond farewells
> to days of old

Starting out
on a new endeavor
Leaving as a gift my well-picked bones

Tomorrow brings
a strong change in the weather
And I'm the focused face of that storm

GIVE ME A STORM

Give me a storm
I'm about to be born
Light the lanterns
and look out below

It is foretold
from the frost and the cold
comes a figure
as bright as the sun

> Child of the storm
> and the lightning has torn
> a hole in the sky tonight
>
> As day arrives
> we emerge from inside
> the thundering heat of your heart

The one who survives
keeps the fire inside
through the darkness
and unending snow

Until the day
when the ice melts away
and I'm born
in the eyes of the young

Child of the storm
and the lightning has torn
a hole in the sky tonight

As day arrives
we emerge from inside
the thundering heat of your heart

Give me a storm
I'm about to be born
Light the lanterns
and look out below

ALL THE BONES

All the bones
at the bottom of the ocean
Rest peacefully
in my dreams

The lost souls
tugged by desperate emotions
Sacrificed
to gravity

> From the ledge
> hear the last fateful message
> Whispering
> in the breeze

I'm going in
I'm going in

Yesterdays
have something they want to tell us
The visitors
in my dreams

From the sky
the horizon lays open
I still hear
the whispering

I'm going in
I'm going in

In Slow Time

In slow time
space unwinds
I'm drowsy
sunk so deep
I'm almost
out of reach
I'm almost
out of reach

The slowdown
as I drown
I'm on the
edge of sleep
I'm almost
out of reach
I'm almost
out of reach

Warm world of indigo
growing darker down below
Warm world of indigo
The surface sparkles
I let it go

In slow time
I feel divine
Satiated
and complete
I'm almost
out of reach
I'm almost
out to reach

DISASTER

I fell
so far
into the morning
It knocked me
senseless
Off of my mooring
Disaster
Failure
It was but a warning
of what's
inside
of me

Drifted
ashore
Wreckage behind me
But surely
I lived
Survived the unwinding
Disaster
Failure
It's so liberating
It's what's
inside
of me

Did I believe
life flows smooth and free?
Did I dream
disaster?
Mercy me

Mother
Ocean
She is still calling
She's waiting
patient
out in the darkness
Disaster
Failure
It all means nothing
It's just
a long
daydream

GOT THE BEATLES

Got the Beatles
under the needle
I think it is
they're saddest song

I am drinking
in slow motion
My buzz will last
all day long

       Of course I dream
       a thousand things
       I'm just no good
       at remembering

       I have a bird
       that only sings
       pretty songs
       when I'm not listening

It smells like rain
in the windows
So I'm opening
all the doors

Let the wind blow
out the cobwebs
that often pin me
to the floor

Of course I dream
a thousand things
I'm just no good
at remembering

I have a bird
that only sings
pretty songs
when I'm not listening

All the forest
misting over
Feels like we're living
in the clouds

Got the Beatles
under the needle
I don't care
if it's too loud

H O W   D A R K   T H E   W A Y

How dark the way
sometimes
how lost
How fierce the wind
and strong
my heart
I walk the night
where shadows flee
Nothing like
I used to be

In softest light
I find
the dawn
A mere mirage
must
carry on
The hunger pangs
the urge to run
Into the fire
of the sun

     Three sharp
     daggers in the heart
     Three sharp
     daggers in the heart
     Tearing
     the old world apart

Marvelous
the threshold
crossed
Twist and turn til
truly
lost

The labyrinth
disorients
Until the way
it makes no sense

With the dimming
before
my eyes
I have no need
to don
disguise
When I return
I will not be
anything
you want to see

> Three sharp
> daggers in the heart
> Three sharp
> daggers in the heart
> Tearing
> the old world apart

How dark the way
sometimes
how lost
How fierce the wind
and strong
my heart
I walk the night
where shadows flee
Nothing like
I used to be

CHIAROSCURO PLACE

And you may say
and you'd be right
that we're all enemies
of natural life

And you may say
we don't deserve
to live another day
We are absurd

    All the more
    I embrace
    my little time in this
    chiaroscuro place
    Chiaroscuro place

And you may say
we don't belong
Shitting on everything
Doing it wrong

And you may say
we're evil beings
Treating each other like
we are just things

    All the more
    I embrace
    my little time in this
    chiaroscuro place
    Chiaroscuro place

I could not see I was
looking at the light
Everything near to me
dark as the night

I had to turn away
Our shadows in disgrace
The light strikes
harshly on my face

All the more
I embrace
my little time in this
chiaroscuro place
Chiaroscuro place

I HAVE BEEN HERE

I leave my marks
where I can see them
      Often in the open
I need to know
I have been here

I walk the world
I stomp the terra
      Swim the seven oceans
Been everywhere
I have been here

Wanna run my hands
   along the curves of your heart
Know the backstories
   behind your works of art
I want to dance
   in the darkest of your thoughts
Want to mingle with your void
   and not be caught

My eyes caress
the long horizon
      Wonder what'll happen
to all of this
I have been here

With the stars
I'm always laughing
        The echoes ring forever
So you will know
I have been here

        I have been here
        I have been running in the meadows
        where the sun lit aspens glimmer
        and the water flows so clear

        I have been here
        Sleeping on the beaches
        where the last remains of summer
        like a sunset disappear

END OF THE WORLD

I am not crying
I'm feeling full
The sky is smoke at
the end of the world

Linoleum patterns
beneath bare feet
I'm stripping down
to what's underneath

Silence
Nobody home
The end of the world
I face it alone

Outside my windows
the world's turning gray
The trees disappear
and so does the day

I make a sandwich
I'll never eat
It's just an echo
how life is now complete

Silence
Nobody home
The end of the world
I face it alone

I'm feeling better
Happy at last
I light a candle
and blow out the match

S U N R I S E

Night sure got the best of me
Tangled in old memories
I can feel the sunrise
coming on

Birdsong in the canopy
Building like a symphony
I can feel the sunrise
coming on

    Wrapped in blankets so alone
    Naked damp cold to the bone
    Sunrise
    please don't be long

    Wide awake this house of ghosts
    Grown so tired of playing host
    Sunrise
    please don't be long

Pressed against the windowpanes
Relieved to see life start again
I can feel the sunrise
coming on

All the fragments of the old
dissolve in brilliant burst of gold
I can feel the sunrise
and I'm gone

SMOOTH

Mostly solo
Smooth in solitude
I love the dim lights
of high aptitude
The hush in the echo
All that's coming through
The font of action
where destiny is tuned

Mostly silent
Waiting for a clue
In the big empty
so one can get through
Meanwhile I'm moving
All I need to do
is all I'm doing
Smooth in solitude

       And I think of summer
       And I see her hair
       Gold and flowing warm as the air

       And I think of twilight
       And I see the stars
       Cold and bright as her eyes are far

Been so hungry
Knew not what to do
Licking the dew drops
I collect from you
Fell into the darkness
and the plenitude
All I am alone
Smooth in solitude

LOVELY LIGHTS

Tell me about the lovely lights
that dance in the darkness of your eyes
On these warm short summer nights
Playing out the fates habits decide

Two traveled time to wind up here
And time will make us disappear
Born to love I sip from life
You are the one on my lips tonight

   Aren't we all but lovely lights?
   Phosphorescence on the waves of life
   We may resemble the stars at night
   that last forever we wish we might

     I am here to learn your secret name
     The one you only know when your heart's ablaze

Aren't we all but lovely lights
Kindred spirits with our fates entwined
Alive for a time to know delight
Show me yours and I'll show you mine

Tell me about the lovely lights
that dance in the darkness of your eyes
On these warm short summer nights
Naked at last nothing to hide

www.ingramcontent.com/pod-product-compliance
Lightning Source LLC
Chambersburg PA
CBHW032217040426
42449CB00005B/638